The Leonardo Trivia Book

by

Lynn Valentine
& Michelle Bubnis

PREMIUM PRESS AMERICA
NASHVILLE, TENNESSEE

THE LEONARDO TRIVIA BOOK by Lynn Valentine and Michelle Bubnis
Published 1998 by PREMIUM PRESS AMERICA
Copyright © 1998 Lynn Valentine

To the best of our knowledge, the information contained herein is accurate and truthful. This book is not authorized or endorsed by Leonardo DiCaprio.

ISBN 1-887654-60-7

Library of Congress Catalog Card Number: 98-67500

PREMIUM PRESS AMERICA books are available at special discounts for premiums, sales promotions, fund-raising or educational use. For details contact the Publisher at P.O. Box 159015, Nashville, TN 37215, or phone toll free (800) 891-7323 or (615) 256-8484.

Cover art by Bob Bubnis
Cover & Interior design by Bob Bubnis/BookSetters
Photos on pages 54 and 63 courtesy of Nashville Photo
The photo on page 78 courtesy of Jack Cardoza. For more behind the scenes photos of *Titanic*, you can go on the internet visit Cricketmedia.com/store/ or Jcardoza@adnc.com.
All other photos courtesy of Photofest
Interior border © 1996 The Learning Company Inc., and its licensors.
Printed by Vaughan Printing

First Edition 1998
1 2 3 4 5 6 7 8 9 10

This book belongs to

_____

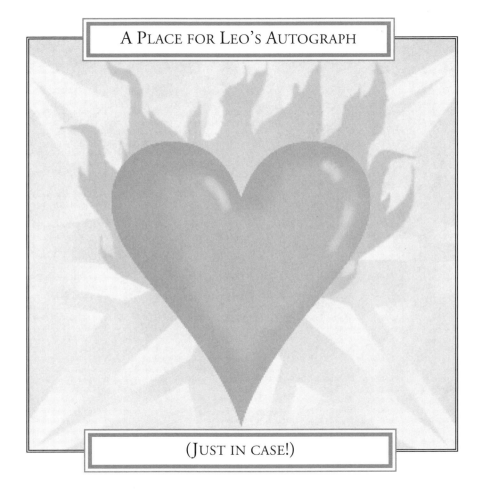

A PLACE FOR LEO'S AUTOGRAPH

(JUST IN CASE!)

DEDICATION

To Mom, Dad, Bob, Shelly, BJ, Mikey, Sparky,
Joe, Lauren, Stacy, Sammie, George, Bette,
Mrs. Rollins and all our friends at WHMS,
everyone at GCF, and Uncle Glen.
Thanks for your confidence.

It doesn't happen often, but once in a great while, a performer comes along that doesn't just entertain us, but somehow in the process of doing their art they change us. These people are the ones that go so far beyond the descriptions *talented*, or *gifted* that they can only be defined as *legendary*. The names James Dean, Marilyn Monroe, Marlon Brando and Elvis Presley fit that category, invoking images in our minds of the young talent of another generation—talent that could not be repressed or restrained by mediocrity and would push the envelope of their abilities instead into history.

Leonardo DiCaprio is one such performer.

While he could have played it safe and relied on his boyish good looks and winning smile to get him less challenging, less controversial, and less commercial roles, (as many others do), DiCaprio looked for parts that were sometimes controversial, sometimes disturbing, but always thought provoking. Through his work we met a tortured poet, a street kid stealing to eat, a mentally retarded boy looking forward to a birthday that the doctors said would never come, and a drug addict, convulsing in the throws of withdrawal. Although there were times we wanted to turn our heads, Leo held our attention, and raised our awareness instead.

Then there are his roles on the other side of the spectrum. With fury and gentleness, his characters took us on romantic journeys, to dream awake of what love should be. Full of passion, his eyes look back from the screen, and in whispers, playful laughter, shouts and sighs, he tenderly tells us the things we want so much to hear. Whether it is as Romeo to his Juliet or as Jack his Rose, his embrace is complete taking us in as well, capturing us in the moment when love finds its expression at last.

Regardless of his role—if as a lover or a fighter, pauper or King, artist or basketball player, poet or cowboy—nearly all of Leo's characters, and Leo himself (by example) encourages us to do one thing above all: To not let inhibition, fear and apprehension steal away our dreams and lull us into complacency. Life is short, and a gift meant to be lived as fully as is possible. Jack said it best in his toast on board the *Titanic*,

"Make it count."

Out of respect for Leo, we purposefully focused on the positive and ignored unsubstantiated or derogatory information. We wanted to include those things that

we felt would best represent Leo and be the most entertaining to you.

As fans ourselves, we could do no less.

So join us now as we embark on a journey through the life of one of film's greatest artists. We hope that you will enjoy reading it, and that throughout its reading you will be surprised, entertained, and inspired by some of what you find in the pages.

Best wishes,

Lynn Valentine and Michelle Bubnis

1. Leonardo Wilhelm DiCaprio was born on November 11, 1974 in Hollywood, California. He was born to be a star!

2. Although Leonardo played the leading man in *Titanic,* the most successful movie in history, he was snubbed by the Academy who did not even nominate him for his role as Jack Dawson. It was another Jack—Jack Nicholson, who took the Oscar home for his work in *As Good as it Gets.*

3. Leo was age 14 when he signed with an agent and was featured in over two-dozen commercials including Matchbox Cars, bubble gum, breakfast cereals, and toys.

4. "It's a frenzy. He has four books on the best seller list and he didn't write any of them."— Oprah Winfrey. (Do I hear *five*?)

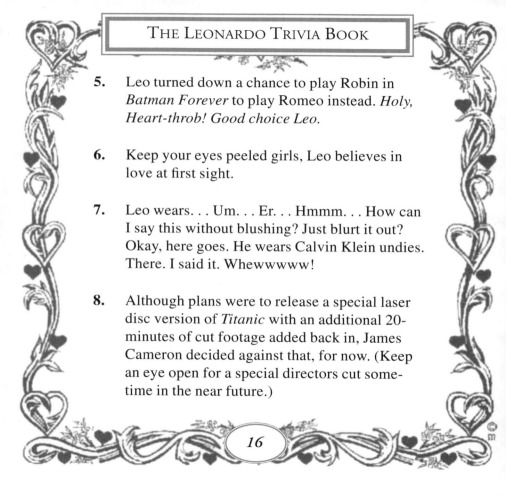

5. Leo turned down a chance to play Robin in *Batman Forever* to play Romeo instead. *Holy, Heart-throb! Good choice Leo.*

6. Keep your eyes peeled girls, Leo believes in love at first sight.

7. Leo wears. . . Um. . . Er. . . Hmmm. . . How can I say this without blushing? Just blurt it out? Okay, here goes. He wears Calvin Klein undies. There. I said it. Whewwwww!

8. Although plans were to release a special laser disc version of *Titanic* with an additional 20-minutes of cut footage added back in, James Cameron decided against that, for now. (Keep an eye open for a special directors cut sometime in the near future.)

9. "When I was young, I used to have this thing where I wanted to see everything. I used to think *how can I die without seeing every inch of this world?*"

10. "DiCaprio was robbed," said Gene Siskel about the Academy's failure to nominate Leo as best actor for *Titanic*.

11. "What are they thinking?" said Roger Ebert about the Academy's failure to nominate Leo as best actor for *Titanic*.

12. Leo's favorite car is a '69 Mustang.

13. "I am just now starting to scratch the surface of what makes me happy, and it has taken me a while to admit that acting like a child and a jerk is fun."

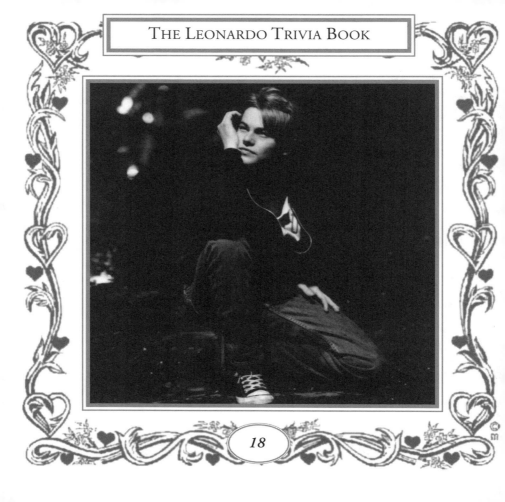

14. Leo kisses Claire Danes twenty-nine times in *Romeo + Juliet*, (two of the kisses are laid softly on her hand.) [sigh]

15. An unconfirmed Hollywood source says *Titanic* did so well financially that James Cameron awarded both Leo and Kate an additional million dollars for their invaluable contribution.

16. A *Titanic* poster was auctioned for $3,105. According to recent news, the autographed poster was consigned to Southeby's Auction House by an anonymous owner. The winning bid was secured in less than a minute. The new owner, George Marciano of Los Angeles, is the founder of Guess Jeans. An unsigned *Titanic* poster accompanied by a black and white signed photo brought $632.

17. Leo's salary for *Titanic*—$2,500,000. Kate Winslet was paid just under a million.

18. The cast (at press time) of Woody Allen's movie *Celebrity*, (in alphabetical order);

> Woody Allen
> Kim Basinger
> Kenneth Branagh
> Saffron Burrows
> Judy Davis
> Leonardo DiCaprio
> Melany Griffith
> Michael Learner
> Joe Mantegna
> Winona Ryder
> Mira Sorvino
> Kate Winslet
> Jeffrey Wright

19. Leo admits that when he's alone with a girl he "does the baby voices, rubbing noses, and you know, the teddy bear thing." Any volunteers?

20. While Leo did a great job playing the artist Jack Dawson in *Titanic*, it was James Cameron's hand that was filmed sketching the picture of Rose wearing the *Heart of the Ocean*. Cameron's hand was digitally enhanced to look somewhat younger, and because Cameron is left handed, the footage was flipped over.

21. Leo's first publicity spot was for Milk. One thing is for sure, milk really did that body good!

22. Titanic Goof-up #1: Jack claims to have gone ice fishing on Lake Wissota. Unfortunately, this lake wasn't created until five years after the *Titanic* sunk.

23. One of Leo's favorite movies is the romantic story of undying love, *Ghost*.

24. "Don't believe everything you read."

25. The going price for Leo's autograph on an 8 x 10 is $45. On a *Titanic* poster it starts at $180!

26. "I've been planted here as a vessel for acting."

27. One of Leo's favorite possessions is a rare baseball card of L.A. Dodger Sandy Kofax given to him by his Dad.

28. Rumor has it that Leonardo prefers brunettes. The main reason for this, sites Leo, is because "there seems to be more of them."(Darn it, I guess there's always hair dye!)

29. Leo's pet peeves include:
1) talk shows
2) false friends
3) actors with hang-ups
4) reporters
5) sleazy producers
6) inflated egos
7) stage parents

30. Although it looked like *Playgirl* was going to do a pictorial of an unclothed Leo, everything worked out for the best in the end, and the objectionable photo's were left unprinted.

31. Titanic Goof-up #2! Leo's character, Jack Dawson, claims to have visited the Santa Monica Pier in California. Unfortunately, the pier wasn't actually built until 1916.

32. Leo requested to replace the late River Phoenix in the role of the interviewer in Neil Jordan's film version of Anne Rice's novel, *Interview with a Vampire.* He auditioned for the part and even though the Director and Producer were impressed, they gave the part to Christian Slater, insisting that Leo was just too young.

33. "Our *Romeo + Juliet* is a little more hardcore and a lot cooler."—Leonardo DiCaprio

34. Leo works out at Gold's Gym in Hollywood. His buddy Mark Wahlberg (don't call him *Marky-Mark* anymore) has been known to work out there as well.

35. Leo's name is on a list to be considered for a wax statue at the world famous Madame Tussaud's Wax Museum in London. It's liable to get hot in there!

36. The blue sapphire copy of the *The Heart of the Ocean,* worn by Celine Dion during her Oscar performance, was recently auctioned for nearly 2.25 million dollars. The money was given to charity.

37. "Leo is the actor of the century"—Kate Winslet

38. Record numbers of girls spent the day with Leo on Valentine's Day 1998! *Titanic* brought in a total 13.1 million dollars on that day alone, surpassing how much it had made even on its opening day!

39. Dozens of girls stopped by a famous coffee beanery near Washington, D.C. each day to see Leo look a-like, Tim Hays. (A.k.a. Leonardo DiCappuccino)

40. "He's the most down-to-earth person I've met. Very un-Hollywood."—Mark Wahlberg

41. When Billy Zane (steel mogul, Caldon Hockley of *Titanic*) was recently asked about his new female fan base, he said, "It's certainly escalated with this movie. Maybe just the leftovers from the Leo craze. I am not sure."

42. Leo donated $5,000 and luncheoned with President Bill Clinton at a Manhattan fund-raiser.

43. The best advice he was ever given, "Avoid obviousness."

43. Leo was on the cover of the May issue of *Teen People,* causing the magazine to sell out in just 10 days. Because the demand was so great, they went back to the presses, printing another 300,000 copies which were rushed immediately to stores across the country.

45. At the Tokyo International Film Festival in Japan, Twentieth Century Fox (*Titanic's* international distributor) provided Leo with 49 security guards. Adoring fans knocked over many of them as they raced over to get a glimpse of Leo, prompting the young actor to say that his fans were among the "Best and most loyal in the world."

46. Leo is great at doing cartwheels.

47. Leo's beautiful face has graced the covers of over 100 magazines all over the world (and my room as well!)

48. Leo's favorite vacation spot is Germany.

49. Leo's first on-screen kiss was on the show *Parenthood* in 1990.

50. In an interview with *Rolling Stone* magazine, Kate Winslet said that she and Leo spent their off hours on location trading tips on the opposite sex. She said, "many of Leo's suggestions have come in handy and I know it's vice-versa."

51. During the shooting of the "I'm the King of the World," scene, Danny (Fabrizio) Nucci recalled how they were supposed to be absolutely enthralled and elated with life in that shot but it was difficult. Danny had to use the restroom and Leo hadn't eaten and was starving. They stuck it out for another 3 1/2 hours.

52. As a child, Leo's favorite musician was Stevie Wonder.

53. "Leo doesn't try to impress anyone. He knows who he is."—James Cameron

54. Leonardo was sued April 14th, 1998 by independent film producer David Stutman and his production company Polo Pictures Entertainment, alleging that Leonardo and Tobey Maguire have been trying to prevent the picture *Don's Plum* from theatrical release. The official statement released by the publicists for Leo and Tobey is as follows: As a favor to a friend and first time director, Leo and Tobey agreed to participate in an experimental black and white short film with an improvised script. Mr. Stutman and R.D Robb secured Leo's participation with the express agreement that it would never be exhibited as a feature-length motion picture. It is incredibly disappointing to find Mr. Stutman attempting to exploit Leo and Tobey by converting Leo's twelve hour favor to a friend into a multi-million dollar studio feature film release. Leo and Tobey stand by their word and are saddened that Mr. Stutman is not standing by his.

55. When Leo goes to the Mall and sees girls following him around, he wonders, "Do they recognize me or do they just think I'm weird?" [Note from the authors; No Leo, they just think you are a righteous babe. I am glad that I can clear that up for you.]

56. *King Kong* was Leo's favorite movie as a child.

57. Leo was a real goof in school. He couldn't really focus on things he didn't want to learn about. He'd break up the day by getting his friends and break dancing and doing skits in front of his classmates at lunchtime.

58. Leo's longest running film to date is *Titanic* at 3 hours and 14 minutes. His shortest is *The Foot Shooting Party,* which clocks in at a mere 27 minutes.

59. Leo loves computers and video equipment.

60. Leo's first film was *Critters 3*. He doesn't like to talk about that one though.

61. When Leo found out that his step-brother, Adam Starr, made $50,000 for a television commercial, that's when he knew that he wanted a career in show business.

62. When asked about her leading man in *Titanic*, Kate Winslet said, "He's probably the world's most beautiful looking man and yet he doesn't think he's gorgeous."

63. Leonardo's pediatrician was Dr. Paul Fleiss. If that name sounds familiar, you are right. He is the father of Heidi Fleiss.

64. Leo spent the summer of 1996 going from one amusement park to another. "I had my ultra-amusement park summer," he says, " I went to Knott's Berry Farm, Magic Mountain, Raging Waters and Universal Studios, three times!"

65. Leo likes to chew shredded bubble gum, (pack-aged like chewing tobacco) and the drink Fruitopia.

66. Leo speaks fluent German.

67. Leonardo said that he took the role in Woody Allen's film *Celebrity* just for the chance to work with the famous director.

68. One of Leo's favorite musicians is Harry Connick, Jr. (You bring the CD Leo, I'll light the candles.)

69. Leonardo's favorite birthday was his 16th, because that was when he learned to drive. His first car was a Jeep Cherokee.

70. Leo's mothers' name is Irmelin. She was born in Germany.

71. Leonardo's favorite actresses are Meg Ryan and Meryl Streep, (the latter he had the pleasure of working with in the film *Marvin's Room*.)

72. Leo's favorite actors are Robert DeNiro and Jack Nicholson.

73. Leo hates being called a hunk. (How about Babe? Is that okay, Leo?)

74. Leo drives a Silver BMW coupe.

75. Leo attended John Marshall High School. One classmate remembered Leo as being "skinny and sorta wimpy looking." (Wonder what that girl is thinking now.)

76. Leo's dreamy eyes are blue-green. He is 6 feet tall and just over 150 lbs. (Oh, and did I mention those dreamy eyes?)

77. Leonardo's favorite sport is basketball. Baseball is a close second.

78. In Italian, the name DiCaprio means "From Capri."

79. "Don't think for a moment that I'm really like any of the characters I play. That's why it's called *acting*."

80. Rapper, Puff Daddy, Leo and Tobey Maguire all scored courtside seats to the NBA All-Star game.

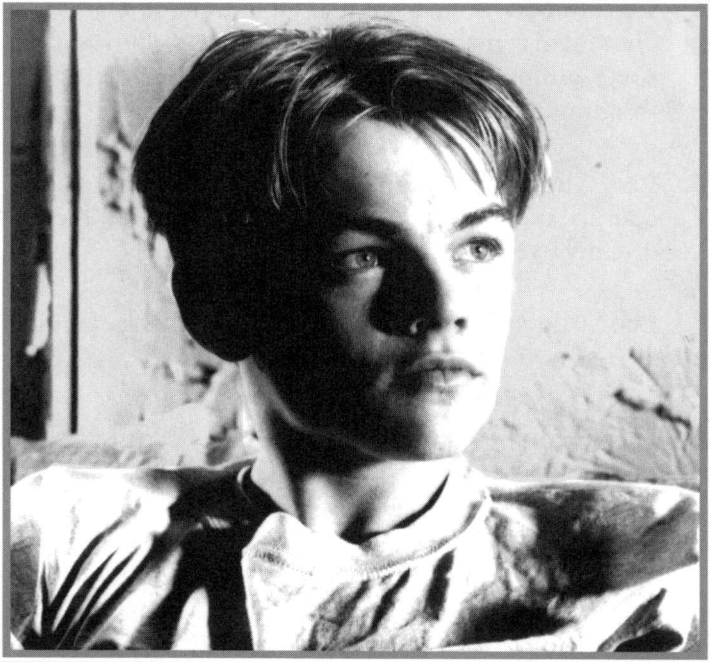

81. Leo says that it doesn't really matter to him whether he wins awards for his performances. The most important thing to him is that *he* feels his work is improving.

82. Leo's least favorite food is meat.

83. Leo was voted "Most Romantic" by *Seventeen* magazine's *True Romance Reader Survey* in the February 1998 issue. Leo was described as "artistic, tortured, and totally gorgeous." (That just about sums him up!)

84. Singer Fiona Apple recently broke up with Leo's good pal, magician David Blain. They had only dated for seven months.

85. Leo used to love to go to thrift shops and buy weird and funky clothes.

86. Leo and Kate Winslet were nominated in the MTV Movie Awards for the "Best Kiss" category. They lost (believe it or not) to Adam Sandler and Drew Barrymore from the film, *The Wedding Singer*. (No offense Adam, but I'm still trying to figure that one out.)

87. Claire Danes, who played Juliet to Leo's Romeo, said, "I spent four months with him and couldn't figure out whether he's really transparent or incredibly complex. I think he's the latter, but I don't know."

88. In Leo's film, *The Foot Shooting Party,* he wears long blonde hair extensions and 70's style bell bottoms.

89. Leo was once rejected for a commercial because they said he had the wrong haircut.

90. Adoring fans send Leo hundreds of hair bands each week (because he said once that he liked wearing them.)

91. Leo loves teasing people. He once joked of Sharon Stone, "She's better than a bag of snot." (Bad picture.)

92. Believe it or not—Leo has never taken an acting lesson in his life.

93. Leo is a big reader! (Quick somebody, get him a copy of this book! P.S. Leo, the authors can be reached by calling the publishers phone number on page 128.)

94. Leo had traveled to Germany seven times before he had turned 10 years old.

95. Leo says "Playing emotionally ill characters gives me the chance to really act."

96. Leo and Kate had become inseparable during the making of *Titanic*, popping in and out of each others trailers. They ate together and were speculated to be romantically involved but they both insisted that they are only good friends.

97. Claire Danes says "Leo is brilliant and very funny." She admits she would "double over with pain from laughing so hard."

98. Leo attended the Hollywood premiere of *Titanic* at Mann's Chinese Theatre on December 14, 1997.

99. One agent actually suggested that Leo change his name to *Lenny Williams*.

100. To help Leonardo feel more comfortable on the set of her nude scene in *Titanic*, Kate Winslet *flashed* him while off-camera. (How's that for an ice breaker?)

101. *Los Angeles* magazine released its list of the most important people under forty. Leo, Kate Winslet and Claire Danes made it. "What we were looking for was talent that has not yet reached its full potential and promises to define the next generation of actors."

102. Leo was not James Cameron's first choice for the part of Jack Dawson. He considered Matthew McConaughey, and Chris O'Donnell (who played Robin in *Batman and Robin*, and the young D'artagnion in *The Four Musketeers*.)

THE LEONARDO TRIVIA BOOK

103. *Titanic* earned 8 Golden Globe Nominations, including Leonardo for best actor.

104. Actress Diane Keaton admitted she was "in love with Leonardo" while shooting *Marvin's Room,* but all he did was make fun of her.

105. Through the Make A Wish Foundation, Leonardo fulfilled the wishes of a group of young girls when he dined with them at the Beverly Hills Planet Hollywood.

106. Even though Leo's parents had split up by the time he had turned one year old, they promised to stay friends and did. The three of them spend time together, and have dinners, go to movies and amusement parks.

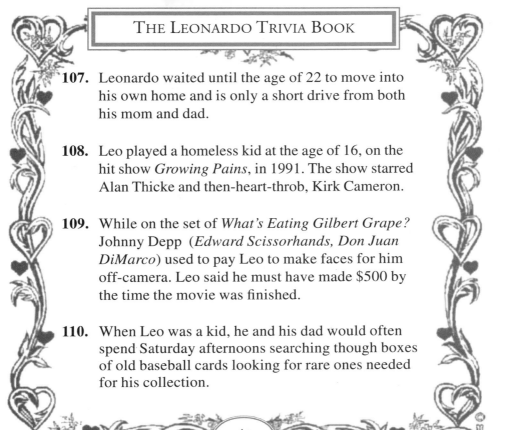

107. Leonardo waited until the age of 22 to move into his own home and is only a short drive from both his mom and dad.

108. Leo played a homeless kid at the age of 16, on the hit show *Growing Pains*, in 1991. The show starred Alan Thicke and then-heart-throb, Kirk Cameron.

109. While on the set of *What's Eating Gilbert Grape?* Johnny Depp (*Edward Scissorhands, Don Juan DiMarco*) used to pay Leo to make faces for him off-camera. Leo said he must have made $500 by the time the movie was finished.

110. When Leo was a kid, he and his dad would often spend Saturday afternoons searching though boxes of old baseball cards looking for rare ones needed for his collection.

111. "At the end of the day I know I've had more fun being famous than I would have otherwise. The attention I'm getting, having people I respect admire me—it's not bad for a kid from east Hollywood!"

112. Leo's manager, Rick Yorn, said in an interview that Leo currently has 15 scripts on hand to read, all of which offer a minimum of $15 million. The one that Leo liked the most was *As I Lay Dying* with Jack Nicholson, and Sean Penn.

113. Leo's nickname is "noodles".

114. Leo's main goal in life is to be a successful actor.

115. One of Leo's favorite restaurants in New York is West Village's *Taka*.

116. Between takes on the set of *Titanic*, Leo would do "dead on" impressions of actors, crew members, and whomever would happen by.

117. Leo loves Life! *Life* is a Club on Bleecker Street in the West Village, famous for its celebrity guests. "When Leo is here," says an employee, "he glides through the room. He's flirty, he's accessible, he's cool. He's not a demanding kind of guy."

118. Leo has a huge collection of $5 sunglasses.

119. Leo's favorite book is Ernest Hemingway's *The Old Man and the Sea*. (The author's favorite is about a *young* man and the sea!)

120. Leo was reluctant to take the role of Romeo, but it was his father George, that persuaded him to take a second look at the script.

121. Leo is a computer whiz, who likes to surf the net. If you like to get on-line too, you might just run into him at one of the following sites, (whom the authors also wish to thank for the information their sites provided).

www.dicaprio.com
www.celebsite.com/people/leonardodica-prio
www.pathfinder.com/people/profiles/leonardo

or, for the official Leonardo home page
www.leonardodicaprio.com

122. "We had the sense that nothing was ever going to stop him. He just lit up the place."—Alan Thicke

123. Leo spent a week in Cuba just to learn more about the countries artists and culture.

124. *Titanic* director James Cameron, admittedly was underwhelmed by Leo's appearance. He didn't want Leo at first to play the part of Jack Dawson. (Can you believe that?) Then Leo got up and read his line, convincing James that he had found his man.

125. In his movies, when he's called to cry in a scene, he only has to think that his mother is in pain and the tears fall.

126. "It's a weird adjustment living alone, because you don't realize how much you miss mumsie until she's not there."

127. Leo says "success hasn't spoiled me, I'm handling it well and haven't gone crazy yet."

128. Kate Winslet missed the Royal Charity Premier of *Titanic* in London after taking ill. The 22-year old actress was taken to a local hospital suffering from flu-like symptoms. After hosting the premier, James Cameron and Leonardo said their goodbyes to Prince Charles and came directly to the hospital to check in on her. Sources reported she miraculously felt better the next day. (Must've been Leo's bedside manner.)

129. Romeo Goof-up #1: The bottle of poison falls from Romeo's hand as Juliet reaches out to touch his cheek, but later she removes it from his hand.

130. Leo loves writing poetry and short stories in his spare time. (What a coincidence, I love reading poetry and short stories in my spare time! How about it Leo!)

131. Leonardo repeatedly shocks the Hollywood community by turning down roles he felt were, "too commercial," or "too mundane."

132. Leo and Kate Winslet have been crowned "Mr. and Ms. Showbiz" in Showbiz's On-Line Annual Pageant.

133. *Total Eclipse* is the 1995 biographical film version of the life of Arthur Rimbaud, a 19th Century poet. It only made $350,000 in its domestic release.

134. Leo is so hot in Paris, that merchants can't keep Leo memorabilia in stock. *Titanic* and Leo items such as stickers, post cards, T-shirts (and hopefully trivia books), are on backorder.

135. Leo and Claire Danes have been voted two of the *20 Hottest Stars Under 30,* by E!Online.

136. Leo's favorite TV shows as a teen were, *Parenthood*, and Will Smith's, *Fresh Prince of Bel Air*.

137. Leo was attracted to the lead role of Jim Carroll in *The Basketball Diaries* because "there's such a ridiculous heroin craze going on right now and it's so sad." This was *his* statement against drugs.

138. As a child, Leo loved dinosaurs. His sixth birthday cake was covered with dinos.

139. *The Quick and the Dead* star Sharon Stone said about Leo, "He is the most gifted young actor I have ever seen."

140. Leo and his close knit group of friends have been known to frequent such night spots as The Whiskey and The House Of Blues in Los Angeles.

141. Old friend and mentor Alan Thicke invited Leo to guest appear on his show *Pictionary,* but Leo had to turn him down because he was too busy at the time. Like a true friend though, he asked Alan to call him again at another time.

142. Back in school, one of Leo's favorite impressions to do was singer Michael Jackson's famous moonwalk. (Which he is still known to do on occasion.)

143. Leo's role in the film *Total Eclipse* was originally offered to the late River Phoenix.

144. Leo was so interested in the ocean as a young child that he wanted to be an oceanographer when he grew up. Little did he know that he would later be forever associated with the ocean, and one of the grandest ships to ever sail it.

145. Leo has never taken drugs.

146. While on breaks from shooting *Titanic*, off duty actors would be rocking out in an impromptu band. Danny Nucci, Billy Zane, and a couple other guys would get together and jam for a couple of hours. Leo would just come in and start singing "I Will Survive" at the top of his lungs to embarrass them.

147. His favorite character in history is John F. Kennedy, for "his fight to end racism."

148. Leo said that he "became a man while filming *Titanic*." (We noticed, Leo!)

149. Although Leo is a multi-millionaire, he is also very frugal. He's been known to look for a place on the street to park rather than use Valet Parking.

150. "I prefer ordinary girls, you know, college students, waitresses, that sort of thing. Most of the girls I go out with are just good friends. Just because I go out to the cinema with a girl doesn't mean we are dating."

151. In 1994, Leo was nominated as best supporting actor for his role of Arnie in *What's Eating Gilbert Grape?* He lost to Tommy Lee Jones for his role as the relentless U.S. Marshal chasing after Harrison Ford in, *The Fugitive.*

152. *The Basketball Diaries* was the first time where he actually read a script and didn't want to put it down.

153. Hoping to get the role in *What's Eating Gilbert Grape?,* Leonardo turned down the role in the Bette Midler film, *Hocus Pocus.*

154. Although he believes in love at first sight, Leo says, "I've never been a romeo, who meets a girl and falls for her immediately. . . it's been a much slower process for me each time I've gone into a relationship."

155. Titanic Goof-up #3: In the scene where Jack is teaching Rose how to spit, he has a clean chin as he begins to turn around to meet Roses mother, but has quite a streak of slobber going when he faces her.

156. "It was closer to manual labor than shooting a film. I always think of something Michael Caton-Jones told me, 'Pain is temporary, film is forever.'"

157. Leo loves Pink Floyd, The Beatles and Led Zeppelin.

158. Romeo Goof-up #2: The wounds on Romeo's face, switch sides at one point in the film.

159. Leo says that if he ever gets tired of acting, he'll go into directing. Whatever he does though, it looks like it's going to be in the movie business.

160. Do you want the good news first, or the bad? Okay, good news first.

Leo said he "definitely wants to have the security that settling down brings." He's "looking forward to getting married and having kids."

Now for the bad news.
"But it's not time for that yet."

(Fine, I can wait.)

161. Leo says that his worst trait is that he procrastinates. (Maybe that's why he hasn't written me back yet!)

162. Leo's first memory is of being lifted onto a stage by his father to entertain people waiting for a concert.

163. Leo was voted one of People magazines, *50 Most Beautiful People in the World*. (In fact, he made the cover of that issue, which, incidentally is pinned up over my bed.)

164. Leo's favorite song is *Sitting on the Dock of the Bay*, by Otis Redding.

165. Leonardo escorted (then) girlfriend, Kristen Zang to the premier of William Shakespeares' *Romeo + Juliet*. He once said she was "the cutest girl in the world." (Wait a minute, you haven't seen me yet!)

166. Leo's favorite drink is lemonade.

167. Leo's favorite colors are black and purple. (Let's see, where did I put that black and purple bathing suit?)

168. Leo is a "natural" blonde.

169. Among Leo's favorite movies are *The Godfather, Godfather Part Two,* and *Godfather Part Three.*

170. Leo has a habit of biting his nails and twisting his hair.

171. Leo used to play the organ.

172. *Newsday* wrote; "[In *Titanic*] DiCaprio has a captivating presence in a role that might have been written for a young Clark Gable."

173. Leo loves to shoot pool and play video games.

174. Leo is a huge L.A. Lakers fan and says he never misses a game when he gets the chance to go.

175. Leo's father, George, will serve as one of the producers in "Bombshell" an espionage thriller for Universal Studios.

176. No wonder Leo has that squeaky clean boy-next-door look. His favorite thing to do as a small child was to take a bath. He used to take his action figures and toy dinosaurs with him.

177. Leo played on the TV show *The Outsiders*, based on the hit movie.

178. Leo's favorite shoes are Black Doc Marten's. He wears a size 11.

179. Leo filmed a guest appearance on the mega hit comedy show *Roseanne*, but later, that scene was cut. (Wrong move, Rosie!)

180. Leo admits that he gets a kick out of imitating the way people walk and talk.

181. Leo played a teenage alcoholic in the television soap opera *Santa Barbara* when he was 15 years old.

182. When he was a child, he was always being mistaken for a girl, because of his long blonde hair.

183. Leonardo loves diet soda.

184. One of Leonardo's favorite childhood memories is terrorizing his neighbors with practical jokes.

185. In *Titanic*, Rose says the name "Jack" 76 times.

186. Leonardo's first date was with a beautiful girl named Cessi. They went to see *When Harry Met Sally*, and then went to dinner. They ordered French Dip Sandwiches.

187. Leo admits that he's done a few lousy roles at the beginning of his career, like his role in *Critters 3*. "But at that age, you'll do anything for attention."

188. DiCaprio loves whales and dolphins. The first place he goes when he gets a break is to the sea.

189. When asked, Leo said that he loved the color green because, "it's the color of nature, the color of money, and the color of moss."

190. Leo loves to eat pasta for dinner. (Okay, so far, things to add to the grocery list are, diet soda, salad, and pasta.)

191. "I'm not really the quiet type, although some people think I am. But I'm the rebel type in the sense that I don't think I'm like everyone else. I try to be an individual." (It worked, there is nobody out there like you Leo!)

192. In 1997, the J. Peterman Christmas Catalog sold the vest, shirt and pair of trousers worn by Leo in *Titanic* for $9,000.

193. *The Man in the Iron Mask* was MGM's widest film release in the studios history (at press date), the film opened in 3,101 locations.

194. Leo's mom said that he was always a very well-behaved boy while growing up. "The only time I ever had to discipline him was when he was little and I told him not to cross the street and he didn't listen."

195. "I hate speaking in front of a large audience. I don't know where it came from. . . but it's just this gut-wrenching fear of slipping up and doing something horrible."

196. According to *The New York Post*, fashion model Vanessa Haydon and Leo reportedly met in the New York apartment of Leo's financial manager Dana Giacchetto, at a party after the premiere of the Robert Downey movie *Three Girls and a Guy.* Rumor's flew around immediately that the two were dating.

197. Leo hates littering and thinks that people should try to recycle whenever possible.

198. While traveling, Leo always packs his Gameboy portable video game system.

199. Leo loves James Dean movies, his favorite is *East of Eden*. When asked if Leo would portray Dean, he told an interviewer, "He's such a colorful actor to get into. I could never really be him. He was such an original, and I'd just be imitating him."

200. When he landed the part of Luke on *Growing Pains*, Leo and his parents celebrated by going out to dinner and going shopping. Leo bought an $80 pair of shoes.

201. Leo always makes his own cards for his Mom on special occasions such as Valentine's Day, Mothers Day and her Birthday. She has saved them all.

202. Tracey Gold of Growing Pains, once said to a reporter "He's a great actor who will definitely go into great movies."

203. Leo appeared in two episodes of *The New Adventures of Lassie.*

204. Leo was offered the leading role in *All the Pretty Horses,* one of the most coveted parts being shopped around in tinsel town. He didn't make up his mind whether or not he wanted to do it in time, so at press time, Matt Damon, (*Good Will Hunting*) is expected to do the picture instead.

205. Siskel and Ebert gave "Two Thumbs Up" to Leo's performance in *This Boy's Life*.

206. Among his favorite places to shop in New York, Leo likes the New York Plaza, Prada, Mossimo, and Barney. In L.A. he goes to Fred Segal's.

207. Leo enjoys watching reruns of *The Twilight Zone*.

208. The first home Leo bought for his mother was in Los Feliz. It came complete with a built-in swimming pool and a ping-pong table in back for her to enjoy. It is said Leo is building a new home for her in North Carolina as well.

209. *Titanic* made its world debut in Japan at the Tokyo International Film Festival in November 1997.

210. Art has always been important in Leo's life. He feels that the art world is the only place left where it's still possible to explore the extremes. (If you would like to check out some of Leo's art, you can do so at the Art Gallery on the Official Leonardo Home Page, found at www.leonardodicaprio.com.)

211. Academy Award winning actress Meryl Streep said, "Leo is always very compelling. . . You can't watch anything else while he's acting."

212. After a long search for the perfect Juliet, it was Leo who was instrumental in casting actress Claire Danes for the part. Leo had seen her work on the series *My So Called Life,* and was so impressed with her that he recommended her to Director Baz Luhrmann.

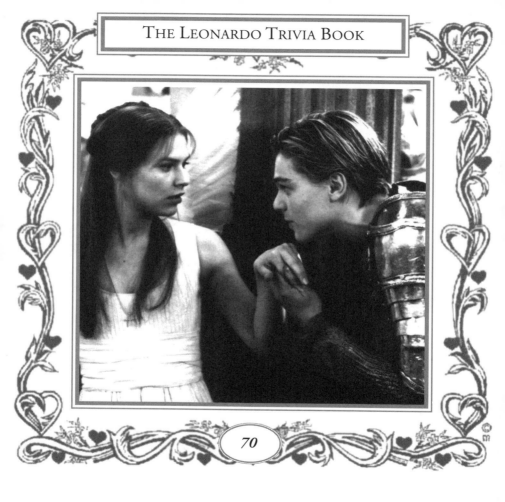

70

213. Leo remembers his humble beginnings and charities have become of big importance to him. He has donated food and clothes to homeless charities, and attended fund-raising benefits for AIDS charities. He's also given generously to the Ronald McDonald House, to the conservation of dying species charities and the Save the Manatees in Florida.

214. Leo's favorite outfit is a T-shirt, jeans and shoes. (My favorite outfit is an oversized *Titanic* shirt!)

215. When Jim Carroll went out to do his book signing tour for *The Basketball Diaries,* Leo, who played Carroll in the film, went along with him to help promote it. Both of them signed the books. (Hey Leo, how about coming along with us to sign this book!)

216. There was a four month casting search for the perfect actor to portray Tobias Wolff in Michael Caton-Jones' emotional true-life drama *This Boy's Life*. Although Leo was among the first of the 400 actors to audition, the cattle call went on from L.A. to N.Y. and everywhere in between, but they just kept coming back to Leo.

217. Leo's biggest wishes are to save the environment and to live in peace.

218. Leo would rather be told he has a great sense of humor, than to be told how good he looks.

219. James Cameron had asked Leo consider the lead role in his long-awaited film adaptation of the comic book *Spider-man*, however, it didn't appear at press time, that Leo would be climbing the walls.

220. Some of Leo's famous friends, are Johnny Depp, Juliet Lewis, Adam Duritz, Sara Gilbert and Mark Wahlberg.

221. One of Leo's favorite passtimes is looking for art in trendy Soho art galleries.

222. Alan Thicke thought Leo was a "really talented kid" especially after he caught Leo doing an impression of him.

223. Leo made two educational films for T.V., *Mickey's Safety Club,* and *How to Deal with a Parent Who Takes Drugs*.

224. Jack Cardoza, an extra in the film *Titanic,* said that Leo was, "friendly and approachable on the set. He was always willing to stop and sign autographs, or pose for a picture."

225. When Leo isn't making blockbuster movies, he likes to get involved in charity work. He scored points knocking pins over at a bowl-a-thon to benefit the *American Diabetes Association.*

226. Of his friend and female lead in *Titanic,* Leo said, "Kate is a terrific, beautiful, great, and talented girl."

227. In October of 1997, Leo ranked #75 in *Empire Magazines* "The Top 100 Movie Stars of All Time" list. (I don't think there is any doubt who will take home the honors the next time.)

228. Early in his career, Leonardo was mistakenly called Leonard, a name he hated! I don't suppose that happens much these days.

229. When Leo was little, his mom was always stopped by people who wanted to look at him. "I always heard a lot of compliments on how good he looked and that he should be in the movies."

230. In between takes on the set of *Titanic* during the sinking, buckets of warm water had to be poured all over Leo to keep his body temperature up.

231. With the mega-movie hit *Titanic*, under his belt, Leo could be the highest paid actor in Hollywood commanding a whopping $25 million per movie, beating out the salaries of top stars like Jim Carrey, Tom Cruise and Arnold Schwarzenegger.

232. The rumors that Leo was dating the beautiful model Naomi Campbell are false. They do know each other, and have been seen at the same celebrity hot spots, but the two have never dated.

233. Leo called Luke (his character on *Growing Pains*) "really charming and a bit of a weasel."

234. Recently, Billy Zane (Cal Hockley in *Titanic*) was mobbed by kids wanting his autograph. All the girls wanted to know what it was like to work with Leo and he said, "Well, since Leo's good looking and talented, it wasn't hard for me to be mean to him," Billy joked. "Actually, I have a lot of respect for Leo because he's such an intense actor who makes interesting choices with his roles."

235. Leo's cameo role in *Poison Ivy*, was so small he wasn't even mentioned in the credits.

236. Legend has it that just before Leo was born, he kicked at the precise moment his mom was looking at a painting by Leonardo DaVinci. Hence the name Leonardo.

237. Leo appreciates all the love he got while growing up and says "I was raised really well. Hopefully, I can raise [my children] the same way."

238. "I really don't know what I'm doing, I don't. It's terrible. I go in there and learn how to be like the character and do the best I can. That's all I really do."

239. The first set of words that Leo said in German were Oma and Opa for Grandma and Grandpa.

240. Kate Winslet said that on the set of *Titanic*, Leo would occasionally scare people with his pet bearded dragon "Blizz". It was Leo, however, that really got the scare when the lizard got loose and was run over by a truck! Thankfully, and to Leo's great relief, his scaly friend only got his tail hurt, and survived the ordeal to scare again another day!

78

241. In the film *Basketball Diaries*, the script called for Leo's character to snort cocaine. To manage this effect, he sniffed ovaltine and used Q-tips to clean his nose afterward. It was all worthwhile in the end though. Not only did he make one of the best anti-drug movies ever, but he also made a million dollars for that role.

242. "If you hear of any incident about me—a fight. . . don't believe it till you talk to me!" (This goes for any girls you might hear he's going out with!)

243. "I always had this feeling. That's the truth, not some nice little fairy tale. I didn't know whether it was going to be in acting or whatever, but I was going to get lucky. I didn't even plan for college because I was determined that it was going to happen."

244. "He is the next James Dean"—Claire Danes

245. On January 18, 1998, at the 55th Golden Globe Awards, Leo drew the loudest screams from the audience. He emerged from a limo with Kate Winslet on his arm. They both looked very glamorous and took the opportunity to sign autographs for the fans lining the walkway.

246. "Leo and Kate got along very well—almost like a brother and a sister," says Jack Cardoza, one of the extras on *Titanic*. "They would often throw playful punches at each other, and even get into fake fist fights."

247. Leo received four nominations for the 1998 MTV Awards. Best male performance, best duo (with Kate Winslet), best kiss (with Kate) and best male breakthrough performance (which he won!).

248. "I like to be able to play a character and act out a lot of things which I can't or don't do in my normal everyday life," Leo has said. "It gives me a legal excuse to go nuts with the character. The more nuts I go and the more I show, the deeper I get into the depression or the happiness or the anger of the character, and the more real it is."

249. Leo was given a tiny set of boxing gloves as an infant by family friends. (Who would have known that he would turn out to be a lover, not a fighter.)

250. When he was a kid, Leo loved the cartoon *Submariner.* (There he goes with the water thing again!)

251. "I was about sixteen when I learned how to flirt and I had a bit of a routine going on." (Hey Leo, it's still working.)

252. Titanic Goof-up #4: If you look over Leo's shoulder in the scene where Jack is strolling along the promenade deck with Rose, you can see a small building on a hill, just over the ship. (You'll notice it if you can tear your eyes off of Leonardo long enough to look for it!)

253. Frustrated from being rejected by countless auditions, Leo almost quit acting. Fortunately for him and for us, his dad came to the rescue and said; "Someday Leonardo, it will happen for you. Remember these words—just relax."

254. "The best thing about acting is that I get to lose myself in another character and actually get paid for it. It's a great outlet. I'm not really sure who I am—it seems I change everyday."

255. Leo spent New Year's Eve with Sara Gilbert and other friends in his posse at the trendy South Beach nightclub *Bash* which is owned by Sean Penn.

256. Leo's favorite hangouts are: *Bash, Miami, Tunnel* and *Life* in N.Y., *Skybar, Barfly,* and *Millennium* in L.A.

257. Leo won Best Male Performer for *Titanic* at the 4th Annual Blockbuster Entertainment Awards. (They are the largest publicly voted awards handed out in the fields of both film and music.)

258. Leonardo refused to go to day care by crying so much that Irmelin, his mother, ended up caring for neighborhood children instead of working outside the home just so that she could keep him home with her.

259. Leo was first given the script to *Marvin's Room* by his idol and *This Boy's Life* co-star, Robert DeNiro.

260. "I like attention and I always strive to be different," Leo said at age 15. Little did he know he'd be the center of attention in the biggest film of all time, countless magazine articles, and more than a few books!)

261. Leo met his best friend Tobey Maguire while auditioning for *Parenthood*.

262. Leo does a great impression of Robert DeNiro. It is so good that he actually did it on the *David Letterman Show* to the delight of his fans!

263. Leo's middle name Wilhelm, is pronounced *Vilhelm*.

264. Leo fans are so obsessed that they take notice of the littlest details. One fan club even went so far as to count the number of times DiCaprio licks his lips, or twiddles his thumbs during interviews. For example, during his spot on *The Late Show with David Letterman,* Leo licked his lips 29 times, twiddled his thumbs five times, played with his hair seven times, tweaks his ear once, snaps his fingers once, claps his hands together two times and checks his watch once. (We double checked those statistics for the sake of accuracy.)

265. *This Boy's Life* made about 8 million dollars in its theatrical run. Since *Titanic* came out, however, video stores accross the country have had to order extra copies of this film to keep up with demand.

266. DiCaprio was named, by *US* magazine in 1998 as "Quite simply the world's biggest heartthrob."

267. Robert DeNiro took Leo out on the town (probably to see how good the kids' impersonation of him was) and according to Leo, they ate a bunch of pies together.

268. When Leo was asked what it was like playing the role of Arnie in *What's Eating Gilbert Grape?* he said, "It was strange, I had pudding on my face; I was dirty; I had a chili-bowl haircut and a weird plastic thing on my lip to make my face look a little distorted. Plus, my character had to constantly burp and gag and laugh loud and scream—all the things my mother always told me not to do! So, it was different but kind of fun."

269. When asked in an interview who he liked kissing best between, Kate Winslet (*Titanic*) or Sharon Stone, (*The Quick and the Dead*) Leo picked Kate, saying that Sharon "hurt his lip."

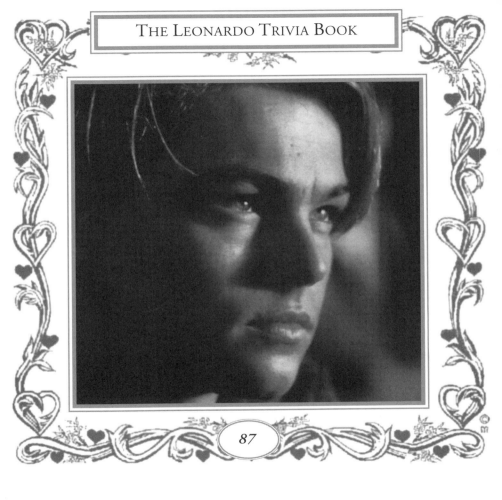

270. Paramount planned the largest marketing campaign in history for the release of the *Titanic* video. The $50 million campaign will include tie-ins with Max Factor and Sprint. Will *Titanic* beat all video sales records as well as box office records? Disney's *Lion King* has sold 30 million copies, and *Snow White and the Seven Dwarfs* topped at 25 million copies with *Independence Day* and *Jurassic Park*, having sold 17 million copies each.

271. Regarding his success Leo once commented, "I've just been jolting along from one film to another. Now, it's sort of a shock to realize what I've achieved."

272. When the readers of *Jane* magazine were asked in a poll who they'd most like to wake up next to, our favorite leading man won by a landslide. (Duh!)

273. *Premiere* Magazine's May '98 issue named the "Top 100 Most Powerful People in Entertainment." They placed Leo on the list at #25, just one spot behind *Men in Black* star Will Smith. James Cameron leapt from #79 on the list last year to # 9.

274. The *New York Daily News* reports that on the night of the Oscar's, Leo and three of his friends were out having a blast in Manhattan eating sushi and clubbing at *Moomba*.

275. Judith Godreche, who played Leo's love interest Christine in the *Man in the Iron Mask*, says that working with Leo was exciting, and kind of scary at first, but she loosened up as they spent time together. "We were rehearsing a lot, talking about our characters, sharing our thoughts. It was nice that he was so young and so romantic in a weird way."

276. The 70th annual Academy Awards, broadcast live on ABC network was watched by an estimated 87 million people in the U.S. That makes it the most-watched Oscar telecast in history. Credit for the huge numbers of course, goes to the intense interest in *Titanic*, which walked away with 11 of the golden statues, including best picture and best director.

277. Judith Godreche, (Christine in the *Man in the Iron Mask)* said that while she had not seen *Titanic* when she started working with him, she understood why Leo was as big a star as he was. "He's an actor so he's the fantasy of a lot of women. But that's normal. He's very handsome and charming and plays very well such a romantic part."

278. Leo's 83-year old grandmother, Helene, resides in Germany. Her grandson's fans carve messages and love letters to Leo on the walls outside her apartment.

279. Leo said of his dual role in *Man in the Iron Mask* , "It's the sort of movie that you dream of being able to make. Every kid has had imaginary sword fights—been a pirate or buccaneer. This was my chance to do all of that with real horses and swords, everything you could imagine. It was really cool."

280. The French magazine *Gala,* said that Leo and model Naomi Campbell were seen swimming in a hotel pool while visiting Havana. (Naomi and Kate Moss were there shooting for *Harper's Bazaar*.)

281. Leo gets his hair colored at Privé Salon in L.A.

282. A comedy that shares the same name with Leo's movie *The Man in the Iron Mask* changed it's name to *The Three Musketeers Meet The Man in the Iron Mask* to avoid confusion. The L.A. Times reports that the film made the change because it seemed that five to ten women per show were complaining that Leo was nowhere to be seen on-screen.

William Richert ,who wrote, directed and starred in the film eventually put up a sign outside the theater that reads. . . "Leonardo DiCaprio is not in this film".

He says that the most complaints were from middle-aged women, and not teenage girls.

283. About Diane Keaton, Leo said, "She has the best laugh in the world, and it's easy to make her laugh."

284. Leo's first acting award was *The New Generation Award* from the Los Angeles Film Critics Association for his role of Toby in *This Boy's Life.* His part in *What's Eating Gilbert Grape?* earned him his second award.

285. While taking a break from shooting *The Man in the Iron Mask,* Leo and his friends were chased by fans at the Lourve in Paris. Later, Leo, his mother and father, and his entourage were given a private tour of the museum. (Which, is the home for many of the paintings of the artist after whom he was named, Leonardo DaVinci.)

286. At the Tokyo Film Festival there were about 2,000 screaming and sobbing fans—some of whom had waited in line for three days and sleepless nights to catch a glimpse of Leo during the *Titanic* premier.

287. The Quigly Poll, which annually asks Theatre owners and exhibitors around the country to name the stars they believe are most responsible for bringing in the most money at the box office put Leo at #3, Julia Roberts at #2 and Harrison Ford at the #1 slot.

288. When Leo is asked to describe himself, he says "I'm shy, but when the time comes to be wild, I am fun-loving, adventurous, and mysterious." [Note to author: Place classified ad reading, "looking for a shy, but wild, fun-loving, adventurous and mysterious man."]

289. "I've always been spontaneous and outgoing. Having fun is a huge priority for me—whatever gets said or written about it."

290. Leo's grandma Helene says Leo "needs to get something on his ribs." She's feels so strongly about it that she is planning a trip to the states to fix that situation. "He'd pass up any hamburger for my apple struesel cake," she says "and for my homemade sauerkraut."

291. While on location in Mexico, Leo was so home-sick for his L.A. friends that he had them flown down to be with him. (He usually has a clause in his contract that enables his pals to fly free to wherever he is filming.)

292. After filming *Romeo + Juliet*, Claire Danes gave Leo a gift of two chocolate eggs and a note saying: "Don't say I never did anything for you, Love Claire".

293. Kate Winslet was already a fan of Leo's and con-
fessed that she longed to play Juliet opposite Leo.
But she adds; "I knew I was too old. The casting of
Claire Danes was brilliant. She's a wonderful
actress."

294. Leo threw his Dad a surprise party for his 50th
Birthday. Just when his Dad bent down to blow out
the candles and make a wish, Leo drove up in a
brand new car and honked the horn. Leo knew his
Dad wanted a new car because all he had driven was
beat up old station wagons. In an interview, Leo
said as he tried to describe his father's expression,
"I couldn't imagine anything more beautiful. . . His
face just lit up!"

295. When Leo was a kid his favorite sweet treat was
ice cream. He now likes lemon bars the best.

296. "I didn't even know what I did in *Gilbert Grape*. I just went off on whatever I felt instinctively without a second thought."

297. "When people ask me 'How do you deal with fame?' I don't have an answer."

298. During the ten weeks of filming *This Boy's Life*, Leo grew four inches taller. At times, he would have to crouch down so as not to be seen taller than Robert DeNiro.

299. Leo's mother drove two hours a day to take Leo to University Elementary School. His father picked him up. (They did it because they wanted Leo to have a better school to go to.)

300. Leo's pet as a kid was a Rottweiler, named "Rocky".

301. "Robert DeNiro is one of the greatest actors who ever lived. That just suddenly hit me when I realized I had the part in *This Boy's Life*. I learned a lot from his professionalism, from his focus. But, I don't work the same way he does. It would take a lot of work for me to get into the role that much. He totally, but totally, is involved in the character. Me? I come in, do the work and walk away so that I can be myself."

302. "I owe so much to my parents and the way I was brought up, but I have sometimes overlooked it— and it's something that I don't want to overlook. The things that you did with them—whether it was spending every Sunday morning with your dad and eating french toast and watching Popeye, or decorating the Christmas tree with your mother—these are the memories that help you to be happy."

303. One of the quickest ways to put a smile on Leo's face is by putting on a movie with one of his favorite comedians. Chris Rock and Jim Carrey are the tops on his list.

304. Leo chose to star in *Total Eclipse* rather than play the legendary James Dean in a Warner Bros. film.

305. Leo inherited his love for pranks and practical jokes from his grandfather.

306. When in Mexico (during the filming *Romeo + Juliet*), Leo reportedly loved the bargain shopping for silver jewelry.

307. Leo went to the premiere of *The Man in the Iron Mask* dateless. (I was available that night Leo.)

308. The *Titanic* soundtrack only fell out of the #1 slot because a new *Titanic* album filled with additional music from the movie and alternative versions of melodies of cuts heard on the first one, was racing up the charts.

309. Leo and others often worked 70 hour weeks while filming *Titanic*.

310. At the wrap party for *Titanic*, Kate presented Leo with a nice thick thermal blanket, since the two of them were both so very cold while filming the scenes in the water. Leo gave her a smile in return. (I definitely know which one of those gifts would warm me the most!)

311. "Leo's favorite music is rap!"

312. Leo says his best quality is his sense of humor. (I think most of us would vote for those eyes.)

313. "He is never too busy to give an autograph or even pose for a picture."—John Landau

314. When Leo has time off one thing he likes to do is make videos starring all of his friends.

315. Leo had moved into a penthouse at The Mercer Hotel in New York, months before it officially opened. His suite is very spacious with more than one view of Lower Manhattan. Inside his room is a marbled bathtub and arched ceilings. The price per night for most rooms is a reasonable $300 plus. The hotel is in the middle of the Soho, surrounded by trendy art galleries.

316. When Leo and Danny (Fabrizio) Nucci would have a couple of hours break from filming on *Titanic*, they would go back to Leo's room and play Nintendo 64 or Sony PlayStation to relax. (No word on who was a better player.)

317. *Moomba* is "The" place to eat in the West Village. It's also the place in which Leo has most often been sited. The menu ranges from Amish Roasted Chicken to Chilean Sea Bass. For desert you can have something called *The Cookie Jar* which is fresh baked chocolate chip cookies and brownies a la mode. Other stars that eat there are Madonna, Kirk Douglas and Boy George.

318. In the early 90's, Leo's agent was Tracey Gold's (Carol Seaver on Growing pains) father.

319. Leo doesn't have a permanent residence in Los Angeles, He's stays in $2000-a-night suites along L.A.'s Sunset Strip. Leo is currently looking for a house to buy for himself in Los Feliz so he can stay close to his mom.

320. To prepare for his role in *This Boy's Life*, Leo was given an educational film about what was "cool" in the 50's. He said "It was strange to see what kids were thinking back then. We look at it now as being ridiculous. But, 20 years from now, the stuff that we're doing and wearing now is going to look just as ridiculous."

321. Leo was fired from the kids' show *Romper Room* when he was only five years old for being too rowdy.

322. Leo's second car is a $35,000 Jeep.

323. Leo said he felt claustrophobic in the iron mask he wore while shooting the Alexander Dumas classic. "It took a long time to feel comfortable in it. I wore it around for awhile and it just becomes a part of you," he says.

324. Katie Holmes, (Joey on *Dawson's Creek*), said that the one dream she'd like to live out is "a date with Leonardo DiCaprio." (Join the club sister!)

325. Before becoming a star, Leo had entertained the idea of being a travel agent or a lawyer.

326. "He's brilliant. I don't know how else to say it. He speaks the absolute truth when he acts, there is not a false beat in him."—Scott Kalvert, Director of *The Basketball Diaries*.

327. According to *Daily Variety*, Leo signed on to do Ernest Hemingway's *A Farewell to Arms* for $22 million dollars.

328. Leo gives all of the credit to *Growing Pains* star Alan Thicke, for teaching him, "how to put the moves on women."

329. After hearing that Drew Barrymore exposed herself on *Late Night with David Letterman*, just days before Leo was scheduled to appear, he groaned, "Oh no! Now I'll be expected to top her. I can't top that. I'm not going to expose myself. What am I going to do?"

330. If Leo could come back as someone famous, it would be "Superman."

331. Leonardo jumps right into charity work. He participated in Pool-Aid 94, which benefited AIDS research. (Kind, cute and generous. You can't ask for more than that!)

332. Leo digs hanging out at fashion shows in both N.Y. and Paris. He's been spotted at several designers' programs including Gianni Versace, Tommy Hilfiger, and Giorgio Armani. He's not only talented and attractive, but he's also got good taste.

333. Leo attended the Royal Premier of *Titanic* in London, on November 18, 1997. He escorted his mother and his grandmother to this grand event.

334. "But soft, what light through yonder window breaks? It is the east, and Juliet is the sun." —Leonardo from Shakespeare's *Romeo + Juliet*.

335. During its opening weekend, we spent $28,638,000. to see *Titanic*. Leonardo's face was seen on 2,674 screens that day.

336. Although the line was scripted, "Lie on that couch," in the scene where Jack prepares to sketch Rose, Leonardo made a mistake and said, "Lie on the bed, uh, I mean couch." Director James Cameron liked it, and used it in the final cut of the film.

337. Although Leo admits he was kind of a goof off at school, eventually he got serious, and while he was being tutored, became a straight "A" student!

338. While he prefers not to eat meat, Leo's favorite fast food (we've heard) is a Jack-in-the-Box turkey, ham and cheese melt.

339. One of Leo's favorite pass-times, is going on the internet and seeing what people are saying about him. No word on whether or not he ever types messages to fans, but watch what you say in those chat rooms girls, he might just be listening in!

340. Leo's favorite character in Star Wars, is Chewbacca the Wookie, Han Solo's faithful, and hairy side-kick.

341. *Party of Five's* Jennifer Love Hewitt said in an interview, "Leo really shines in *Titanic*. . . I cried from the first 20 minutes on."

342. Leo and James Cameron worked on another film together. The *Titanic* director had a cameo part in *The Basketball Diaries*.

343. Leo is so addicted to excitement and adventure that he tried sky diving once. After his parachute failed to open, (his instructor helped and drew the cord on his emergency chute) he began to rethink that sport as an outlet for his energy. He made a video afterward that opened with him saying to himself; "Leonardo, if you're watching this, this is your last time skydiving. It's your first life and death experience and I want you to learn something from it."

344. Leo's dad, George DiCaprio is a former comic-book distributor and his mother is a former legal secretary. They have both *always* been proud parents.

345. In the 4th Annual Blockbuster Entertainment Awards, the fans cast over 15 million votes putting Leo in the top spot, and giving Billy Zane the win for Best Supporting Actor, in *Titanic*.

346. Titanic Goof-up #5: The paintings that Jack was admiring in Roses room; "Les Demoiselles d' Avingnon," by Picasso and "Water Lilies" by Caude Monet, were never aboard the *Titanic*.

347. *Titanic* was Leonardo's first million-dollar (plus) paycheck.

348. In 1990, Leo taped a self-interview where he asked himself, "So, what are your future plans Mr. DiCaprio?" To which he answered himself, "To star in the biggest movie of all time and make millions of bucks doing it."

349. Leo's message of love to his fans—"Try to enjoy life. Be happy. And *always* be yourself. That's basically it."

Critters 3
(1991)

Leo doesn't even like to admit that he had anything to do with this project. It's your basic B-movie with fairly lame effects, but it was the first step on a road that would lead to Titanic achievements.

Cast

Josh	Leonardo DiCaprio	Mr. Menges	Bill Zuckert
Annie	Aimee Brooks	Charlie	Don Opper
Clifford	John Calvin	Terrance Mann	Ugi
Marcia	Katherine Cortez		
Frank	Geoffrey Blake		
Rosalie	Diana Bellamy	Director	Kristine Peterson
Briggs	William Hunt	Story	Rupert Harvey
Mrs. Menges	Frances Bay	Screenplay	David J. Schow

Poison Ivy
(1992)

This is another film that Leo would rather not have on his resumé, because his contribution amounted to only a few brief moments of screen time. Still, it brings us closer to the time when Leo would move into the kinds of roles that would make him legendary.

Cast

Guy	Leonardo DiCaprio	Man in Car	Michael Goldner
Darryl	Tom Skerrit	Dave	George Haynes
"Cooper"	Sara Gilbert	Boy #2	Daniel Gullahorn
Ivy	Drew Barrymore		
Georgie	Cheryl Ladd	Director	Katt Shea Ruben
Bob	Alan Stock	Story by	Peter Morgan
Isabelle	Jeanne Sakata		Melissa Goddard
Kid	E. J. Moore	Screenplay	Andy Ruben
Another Kid	M. B. Quon		Katt Shea Ruben

This Boy's Life
(1993)

This would be the movie that got things started for Leo in terms of critical acclaim and choice roles. In this film, he plays Tobias Wolff, a teenager from a broken family who is beginning to travel with the wrong kinds of kids. His mom, (Ellen Barkin), gets involved with a man (Robert DeNiro) who she hopes will become the father figure Toby needs. Instead he turns out to be a physically abusive tyrant.

Cast

Toby . . . . Leonardo DiCaprio
Dwight . . . . Robert DeNiro
Caroline . . . . Ellen Barkin
Arthur Gayle. . . . . Jonah Blechman
Pearl. . . . . Eliza Dushku
Roy . . . . Chris Cooper
Norma. . . . . Carla Gugino
Skipper . . . . Zack Ansley

Kathy . . . . Tracy Ellis
Marion . . . . Kathy Kiney
Arch Cook . . . . . Bobby Zameroski
Chuck Bolger . . . . . Tobey Maguire

Director. . . . . Michael Caton-Jones
Book by . . . . Tobias Wolff
Screenplay . . . . Robert Getchell

What's Eating Gilbert Grape?
(1993)

In this incredibly good, and award-winning film, DiCaprio turns in a delightful, funny and stirring performance as the mentally retarded Arnie Grape. Playing opposite Johnny Depp, it is the story of a small town family, finding the difference between just living and being alive.

Cast

Arnie Grape. . .	Leonardo DiCaprio	Mr. Lamson.	Tim Green
Gilbert Grape	Johnny Depp	Mrs. Lamson.	Susan Loughran
Beckie	Juliette Lewis	Minister	Rev. R.B. Hedges
Betty Carver . . .	Mary Steenburgen	Todd	Mark Jordan
Mama.	Darlene Cates	Doug.	Cameron Pinley
Amy	Laura Harrington	Sheriff Ferrel	Brady Coleman
Ellen	Mary Kate Schellhardt	Deputy	Tim Simek
Mr. Carver.	Kevin Tighe		
Tucker	John C. Reilly	Director	Lasse Halström
Bobby	Cripsin Glover	Novel by.	Peter Hedges
Grandma	Penelope Branning	Screenplay	Peter Hedges

116

The Foot Shooting Party
(1994)

In this short film, (only 27 minutes), Leonardo plays a singer in the '70's who, during a party with his friends, considers shooting himself in the foot, rather than going to fight in the Vietnam war.

Cast

Star . . . . Leonardo DiCaprio

Director . Annette Haywood-Carter
Screenplay . . . . . Kenneth F. Carter

The Quick and the Dead
(1994)

In this western, Leo again shows his adeptness at portraying fun, interesting, and yet vulnerable characters. He plays Kid, the illegitimate son of Harod, a master gunslinger, and the wealthy wicked "owner" of the town of Redemption. He stages a gun-fighting contest that pits him against a shadow of the past, and his own son.

Cast

Kid	Leonardo DiCaprio	Horace	Pat Hingle
Ellen	Sharon Stone	Katie	Olivia Burnette
Harod	Gene Hackman	Sears	Mark Boone Junior
Cort	Russell Crowe	Mattie	Fay Masterson
Dog Kelly	Tobin Bell	C. Moonlight	Woody Strode
Doc Wallace	Roberts Blossom	Marshall	Gary Sinise
Eugene Dred	Kevin Conway		
Sgt. Cantrell	Keith David	Director	Sam Raimi
Ace Handon	Lance Henriksen	Writer	Simon Moore

The Basketball Diaries
(1995)

This is Leo at his best in the moving true story of Jim Carroll, a promising basketball star that takes a detour off court to go through the depths of despair, depravity and drug addiction. It is an excellent testimony of what the life of a drug addict is like, and after watching Leo's incredible performance, it is hard to imagine anyone contemplating going down that same road.

Cast

Jim Carroll	Leonardo DiCaprio	Diane	Juliette Lewis
Jim's mom	Lorraine Bracco	Bobby	Michael Inperioli
Pedro	James Madio	Reggie	Ernie Hudson
Neutron	Patrick McGaw	Manny	Manny Alfaro
Mickey	Mark Wahlberg		
Swifty	Bruno Kirby	Director	Scott Kalvert
Iggy	Jimmy Papiris	Book by	Jim Carroll
Tommy	Ben Jorgensen	Screenplay	Bryan Goluboff

Total Eclipse
(1995)

Turning down the chance to play James Dean, Leo opted instead to portray Arthur Rimbaud, a 19th century French poet in the midst of a turmultuous relationship with another poet of that time, Paul Verlaine (David Thewlis). Once again, as with his other roles, he brought a level of intensity to this part that few actors would have been able to match.

Cast

Rimbaud	Leonardo DiCaprio	Arthur's Mother	Nita Klein
Paul Verlaine	David Thewlis	Frederick	James Theiree
Isabelle	Dominique Blanc	Vitalle	Emanuele Oppo
Mathilde	Roman Bohringer	Director	Agnieszka Holland
Cabarbaye	Felicie Pasotti	Screenplay	Christopher Hampton

Romeo + Juliet
(1995)

Shakespeare had never been done with quite this twist or look before. Using the poetic words of the original tragedy, and placing the characters in our times, a new generation was introduced to this famous tale of two star-crossed lovers.

Cast

Romeo . . . . Leonardo DiCaprio	Father Laurence . . Pete Postlethwaite
Juliet . . . . Claire Danes	Felgencio Capulet . . . . Paul Scorvino
Marcucio . . . . Harold Perrineau	Gloria . . . . Diane Venora
Balthazar . . . . Jesse Bradford	
Captain . . . . Vondie Curitis-Hall	Director . . . . Baz Luhrmann
Ted Montague. . . . . . Brian Denehy	Play by . . . . . . William Shakespeare
Tybalt . . . . John Leguizamo	Screenplay . . . . Craig Pearce
Caroline . . . . Christina Pickles	Baz Luhrmann

FILMOGRAPHY

Marvin's Room
(1996)

Friend, and Co-producer Robert DeNiro, brought in Leo for this project putting him on screen with Meryl Streep, and Diane Keaton. In this highly acclaimed drama, Leo plays a troubled young man who could be the only hope for an Aunt (Keaton) desperately in need of a bone marrow transplant. More than anything else though, it is a story of reconciliation, redemption, and resolution.

Cast

Hank	Leonardo DiCaprio	Ruth	Gwen Verdon
Lee	Meryl Streep	Charlie	Hal Scardino
Bessie	Diane Keaton	Bob	Dan Hendya
Dr. Wally	Robert DeNiro	Director	Jerry Zacks
Marvin	Hume Cronyn	Based on the play by Scott McPherson	

Titanic
(1997)

It was the most expensive and most successful film ever made, about the grandest ship that ever sailed. This story, about greed, arrogance, commitment and undying love, has broken all the records and catapulted its stars into superstar status. For Leonardo it marks another turning point in the career of a great artist.

Cast

Jack Dawson	Leonardo DiCaprio	Capt. E.J. Smith	Bernard Hill
Rose	Kate Winslet	J. Bruce Ismay	Jonathan Hyde
Cal Hockley	Billy Zane	Spicer Lovejoy	David Warner
Rose (present times)	Gloria Stuart	Thomas Andrews	Victor Garber
Molly Brown	Kathy Bates	Fabrizio DeRossi	Danny Nucci
Brock Lovett	Bill Paxton	Director	James Cameron
Ruth DeWitt Bukater	F. Fisher	Screenplay	James Cameron

The Man in the Iron Mask
(1998)

Leo takes on a different challenge yet, playing opposite himself in this Alexander Dumas classic. Playing King Louis the XIV and his twin brother, not only gave us twice the Leo for the buck, it also gave Leo the opportunity to play two completely diverse and complex characters. One twin, the King, is a merciless tyrant, and the other, Philippe is gentle, and kind, but exiled behind an iron mask.

Cast

King Louis	Leonardo DiCaprio	Queen Mother	Anne Parillaud
Philippe	Leonardo DiCaprio	Christine	Judith Dodreche
Aramis	Jeremy Irons		
Athos	John Malkovich	Director	Randall Wallace
Porthos	Gerard Depardieu	Book by	Alexander Dumas
D'Artagnon	Gabriel Byrne	Screenplay	Randall Wallace

SELECTED BIBLIOGRAPHY

Leonardo DiCaprio, Douglas Thompson, Berkley Boulevard Books, 1998

Leonardo DiCaprio, Modern Day Romeo, Grace Catalano, Bantam, Doubleday Dell Books for Young Readers, 1998

The Leonardo DiCaprio Album, Brian J. Robb, Plexus Publishing Limited, 1998

Lovin' Leo, Stephanie Scott, Scholastic Inc., 1998

Leonardo DiCaprio: A Biography, Nancy Krulick, Archway Paperback/Pocket Books, 1998

Leonardo DiCaprio Romanic Hero, Mark Bego, Andrews McMeel Publishing,1998

James Cameron's Titanic, Twentieth Century Fox, Harper Collins, 1997

Leonardo, A Scrapbook in Words and Pictures, Grace Catalano, Bantam, Doubleday Dell Books for Young Readers, 1998

Leonardo DiCaprio, Fanzine International Inc., 1998

SELECTED BIBLIOGRAPHY

Soap Opera Update Leonardo DiCaprio, Bauer Magazine L.P. 1998

Teen Beat, The Sterling/Macfadden Partnership, various issues

Teen, Peterson Publishing Company, various issues

People Weekly, Time Inc., various issues

16, The Sterling/Macfadden Partnership, various issues

Bop, Laufer Publishing Company, various issues

And a special thanks to all the Leo fans that devoted their time to posting information on the many Leonardo Web sites.

ON SALE NOW!

This book covers the history of the *Titanic*, and provides fascinating facts on all the movies made about this ship's journey into history. Ask for it at your favorite gift or book store, or you can order it from the following page.

Premium gift books from PREMIUM PRESS AMERICA include:

❖ ❖ ❖

TITANIC TRIVIA

❖

BILL DANCES TREASURY OF
   FISHING TIPS

❖

THE LEONARDO TRIVIA BOOK

❖

GREAT AMERICAN COUNTRY
   MUSIC

GREAT AMERICAN STOCK CAR
   RACING TRIVIA

GREAT AMERICAN WOMEN

GREAT AMERICAN GOLF

GREAT AMERICAN CIVIL WAR

I'LL BE DOGGONE

CATS OUT OF THE BAG

❖

STOCK CAR TRIVIA ENCYCLOPEDIA

STOCK CAR FUN & GAMES

STOCK CAR DRIVERS & TRACKS

STOCK CAR LEGENDS

❖

AMAZING ARKANSAS

ABSOLUTELY ALABAMA

FABULOUS FLORIDA

GORGEOUS GEORGIA

TERRIFIC TENNESSEE

VINTAGE VIRGINIA

To order or for more information contact:

PREMIUM PRESS AMERICA
P.O. Box 159015
Nashville, TN 37215-9015
(800) 891-7323
(615) 256-8484 office
(615) 256-8624 fax

PREMIUM PRESS AMERICA books are available in bookstores and gift shops everywhere. If, by chance, none are carried in you local area books can be ordered direct from the Publisher. All premium books are $6.95 plus $2.00 for shipping & handling. Quantity discounts are available. Expect delivery in 7-10 days.